YOUR BEST CAR

*A Step-by-Step Guide To
Buying The Right Car For You*

Shaun R

JONES MEDIA
PUBLISHING

Jones Media Publishing
10645 N. Tatum Blvd. Ste. 200-166
Phoenix, AZ 85028
www.JonesMediaPublishing.com

Disclaimer:

The author strives to be as accurate and complete as possible in the creation of this book, notwithstanding the fact that the author does not warrant or represent at any time that the contents within are accurate due to the rapidly changing nature of the Internet.

While all attempts have been made to verify information provided in this publication, the Author and Publisher assume no responsibility and are not liable for errors, omissions, or contrary interpretation of the subject matter herein. The Author and Publisher hereby disclaim any liability, loss or damage incurred as a result of the application and utilization, whether directly or indirectly, of any information, suggestion, advice, or procedure in this book. Any perceived slights of specific persons, peoples, or organizations are unintentional.

In practical advice books, like anything else in life, there are no guarantees of income made. Readers are cautioned to rely on their own judgment about their individual circumstances to act accordingly. Readers are responsible for their own actions, choices, and results. This book is not intended for use as a source of legal, business, accounting or financial advice. All readers are advised to seek services of competent professionals in legal, business, accounting, and finance field.

Printed in the United States of America

ISBN-13: 978-1-945849-60-2

CONTENTS

CONTENTS

INTRODUCTION

Do you regret your last car-buying decision? Don't want to make the same mistake again? This book will help make sure the next vehicle you buy is the best car for you.

When shopping for a car, it's easy to set your heart on a certain one before you've explored and experienced the other models that meet your criteria. What if there's a better option out there? It's more likely than not that there isn't just one feasible option within your budget or price range, and the step-by-step guide in this book will lead you through the process of finding and assessing the other options. With the tips and tricks included—and one surefire secret to giving yourself the best possible chance of success—you'll be on your way to the most informed car-buying decision you'll ever make. So grab a pencil or pen and let's get started!

1ST) CAR BODY STYLE

Take a moment to think about the purpose of the car you'd like to buy. For instance, will it be for personal or family use? Work? Pleasure? Long trips? Once you've determined the purpose, write it down here: _____.

Now consider what car body styles you're interested in. Sedan?

Coupe? Convertible? SUV? Pickup? Something else? More important, determine which body style will meet your requirements. Do you need a certain amount of passenger space? If so, write your ideal passenger count here: _____. This number will help you narrow down the style options. For example, if you require space for five passengers (or five seats), you can rule out a coupe, but a sedan, an SUV or a van might be the perfect choice. Whatever your style preferences are, write them here: _____, _____. If you're unsure of what the various car body styles consist of, you can look them up on the Internet.

2ND) PRICE

The price of a car usually isn't the total cost of ownership. That figure typically doesn't include sales tax, title or registration fees or any other add-on fees that may be applicable. And then there are the costs of car insurance, yearly registration and taxes, maintenance and fuel. Buyers don't always take these ongoing expenses into account and end up with an additional burden they weren't expecting.

We'll cover insurance and maintenance costs later, but to find out the sales tax rate, you can contact a local dealership or do an Internet search. Knowing the percentage will help you to determine your price limit. Similarly, you can find out the registration-related fees as well. If you aren't able to research these costs, you can estimate them to be about 10 percent of the price of the car (when buying in the United States). (Please note, actual costs may vary.)

How you're planning to pay—financing, leasing or by cash—will also be a factor in your price limit. If paying cash, what price range are you comfortable with? Write the amount here: $_____. If you plan to trade in your current car, you can adjust the pricing accordingly, depending on whether your car has been paid off or there's a balance. To determine the trade-in value of your car, you can visit a local dealership or do an Internet search for "car trade-in value."

If you decide to finance or lease, determine what your comfortable monthly payment is, taking the ongoing add-on costs mentioned earlier into account. Write the amount here: $_____. Now let's calculate your monthly payment based on your price range/limit (from earlier). If you're unsure how to calculate this, go to the internet search for car/ auto loan or payment calculator. Once, determined, write down your preferred monthly payment $_____ and corresponding price range (if different than before) $_____. ★*Tip: When shopping for a new car, to find out the price look for the "Total Price" on the window sticker.*

Note: When buying an electric or hybrid car, consider finding out the costs related to battery replacement, as this can be a significant expense over time. Also, consider at-home battery charging related power upgrades (as necessary) and costs associated with that.

3RD) NEW OR USED

There are several factors to consider in deciding whether to buy a new car or a used car: price, resale value, peace of mind, condition, mileage, warranty, insurance and length of time you want to keep the car. Take a moment to think about which of these factors are most important to you.

Generally, a new car incurs greater depreciation than a used car in the first years after purchase. If you're planning on keeping your car long term, buying a new car could be a better option. However, if the plan is short-term, buying used would be a better option, mainly because of the relatively low depreciation that will occur while you own it.

If peace of mind is an important factor, consider aspects that are important to you. Maybe reliability, a great warranty and low maintenance are things that let you rest easily. To determine a model's reliability, do some Internet research and ask owners of that model about it. As for warranties, generally all new and certified pre-owned cars come with them, but the warranty period and coverage can vary. Warranty information can be obtained from the dealership or the seller. Depending on how old a used car is, it may still have some warranty coverage left. ★*Tip: If you decide to buy a used car, it's suggested that you buy one whose warranty hasn't expired. Also, verify whether there's an option for an extended warranty, which can be a plus.*

If you buy used, it's recommended that you obtain a vehicle history report. You can do this yourself by searching "vehicle history report" on the Internet, or ask the dealership for one (as applicable). A vehicle history report should provide important information related to vehicle history regarding things like previous registration, accidents/damage and maintenance so that you can make a sound decision. ★*Tip: It's also suggested that you have a multi-point vehicle inspection performed on a used car. The inspection should provide you details of a thorough assessment of the car.*

4TH) MAKE

There are so many makes and models out there that it's almost impossible to check out every option that meets our criteria. Yet we tend to form opinions even about the ones we've *never* checked out. You may have heard that certain makes or models have a positive or negative reputation, but the fact is, there's no substitute for experience. Until you've actually driven a particular car, it's best to reserve judgment. ★*Tip: Don't form an opinion about a certain make and model until you experience it. It's only fair to give it a test drive.*

So consider exploring makes and models within your search criteria that you haven't explored before. Check out reviews and forums on the Internet, and talk to owners of those cars. ★*Tip: Regardless of your perception or opinion, don't hesitate to check out a car in person. This will give you a more informed perspective.*

Write down the makes you're interested in here (if you're unsure, leave the spaces blank):

——————————, ———————————,

———————————.

5TH) FUEL TYPE

There are several fuel types to choose from—gasoline, electric, diesel, hybrid—some of which are more common than others. When it comes to choosing among the types, it's about your preference. If you have a preference, write it down here: _____. ★*Tip: If you prefer a hybrid or an electric car, consider researching the costs related to battery replacement, as this can be a substantial expense in the future.*

Fuel economy varies from vehicle to vehicle and can be an important factor when it comes to buying a car. Measured in miles per gallon (mpg) or liters per 100 kilometers (L/100 km), gas mileage has improved over the years. For new cars, fuel economy ratings are typically listed on a car's window sticker. Note: It's possible that your actual gas mileage will vary when compared with the car's mileage rating. ★*Tip: A higher mpg rating indicates better fuel economy, but it's the opposite for L/100 km ratings—a lower rating indicates better fuel economy.*

6TH) OTHER IMPORTANT FACTORS

Take a moment to think about other factors that are important to you. Your list might include any of the following: comfort, driving experience, performance, interior/ exterior design, fuel economy, particular features or options, reliability. Write down the three factors that are most important to you, in order of importance (if you list fewer than three, that's fine):

_____, 　　 _____,

_____.

7TH) MAKING THE SELECTION

Now it's time to start shopping. You can use the Internet to search "car finding," "car buying" or "car trader." Explore at least two of the websites from the results, and look for sites that offer an advanced search or more search options or filters. These options/links might appear in smaller text, so you may have to look closely to find them. Certain filters become available after the advanced search has been initiated. You can choose filters such as "make/model," "body style," "price," "new," "used" and "zip code."

It's suggested that you start your search with the body style you selected in Step 1. If you want to search more than one style, you should be able to select the second or third style by using the filters that become available after the initial search. These filters can be found toward the top of the page.

Now, using the filters, add or select the price range/limit you chose in Step 2. The range may have already been selected when the search was begun. If not, use the filter to select a minimum price and a maximum price. This will help with narrowing down the selection. ★*Tip: You can later adjust the minimum and maximum prices to explore a wider range of selections.*

To narrow the search further, you can select the filter for "used," "new" or both. And other filters should be available as well, such as "make." If you listed makes in Step 4, you can select them here. ★*Tip: It's suggested that, using the steps above, you also explore makes and models other than the ones you've chosen, both online and in person. You may find a better car than you've been looking for.*

Once you've narrowed down your search to just a few cars you're interested in, use the scoring table on page 26 to help narrow it down to a single car—the car that's the best possible choice for you. Here are a few guidelines for using this table:

⇨ Take this book with you when car shopping, and feel free to take notes as desired in the notes section on Page 35.

⇨ In the space provided, write down the year, make and model only of the cars you're considering buying (after checking them out in person and ideally doing a test drive).

⇨ On a scale of 1 to 5, rate the cars based on the criteria listed at the left of the table, with 1 being the lowest score and 5 being the highest, by drawing a circle around the number.

⇨ If you would like to skip an item on the list, skip it for *all* the cars.

⇨ Rate all the cars (up to a total of three cars) for each criterion that hasn't been skipped.

⇨ In the space provided, insert two criteria of your own if you desire.

⇨ Once you've finished scoring all the cars, calculate the sum of the circled numbers in each vertical column and write those total scores in the space provided. The car that receives the highest score is the winner!

Shaun R

	Year: Make: Model:	Year: Make: Model:	Year: Make: Model:
Price	1 2 3 4 5	1 2 3 4 5	1 2 3 4 5
Safety	1 2 3 4 5	1 2 3 4 5	1 2 3 4 5
Comfort	1 2 3 4 5	1 2 3 4 5	1 2 3 4 5
Drive Experience	1 2 3 4 5	1 2 3 4 5	1 2 3 4 5
Performance	1 2 3 4 5	1 2 3 4 5	1 2 3 4 5
Interior Design	1 2 3 4 5	1 2 3 4 5	1 2 3 4 5
Overall Feel	1 2 3 4 5	1 2 3 4 5	1 2 3 4 5
Fuel Economy	1 2 3 4 5	1 2 3 4 5	1 2 3 4 5
Features & Options	1 2 3 4 5	1 2 3 4 5	1 2 3 4 5
Quality	1 2 3 4 5	1 2 3 4 5	1 2 3 4 5
Exterior Design	1 2 3 4 5	1 2 3 4 5	1 2 3 4 5
Passenger space	1 2 3 4 5	1 2 3 4 5	1 2 3 4 5
Trunk space	1 2 3 4 5	1 2 3 4 5	1 2 3 4 5
(Add your own)	1 2 3 4 5	1 2 3 4 5	1 2 3 4 5
(Add your own)	1 2 3 4 5	1 2 3 4 5	1 2 3 4 5
Total Score			

Quick Notes: (Take notes as you please) _____

_____

_____

_____

_____

_____

_____

_____

Your Best Car

_____

_____

_____

_____

_____

_____

_____

_____

_____

_____

_____

_____

_____

_____

_____

_____

_____

_____

Now that you've probably selected a car, here's a suggestion for finding the best deal: Go to a couple of the car websites you searched earlier and filter by specific make and model (try not to apply other filters when initiating this search). Using the sort option (usually toward the top of the page), choose "lowest price" or a similar choice. This should show you the lowest price available. Repeat these steps on another car website.

★*Tip: Expanding the car-search radius or location (typically the distance from a certain zip code) can show you more deals. This can be done by adjusting the radius or location filter. If you find the best deal a long distance from home, you can have the car shipped (this may incur extra cost)*. Sometimes great discounts are offered on year-end models. And for added confidence, look for car-pricing guides on the Internet that will show you the fair price for a given car. ★*Tip: Before financing a car, determine what interest rates you qualify for. You can find this out through your bank or other online sources and obtain preapprovals to ensure that the dealer gives you the best deal available to you.*

You can also determine insurance-related costs by contacting your insurance company and getting a quote or an estimate. Also, based on the car's make, you can contact the service department of the dealership to get an estimate of maintenance-related costs. (This isn't necessary if a maintenance plan is included with the purchase.)

★*Tip: Check back over the notes you wrote in previous steps to make sure they've all been considered as part of the selection process.*

THE SECRET AND OTHER HELPFUL TIPS

Here's the promised secret to successful car-buying: Before buying the car you've selected, rent the same model for at least a day (two days is preferred). Once a car is bought, it typically can't be returned for a full refund. So while a rental is an added cost, it allows you more time than a test drive for exploring that car that you probably can't return. Drive it the same way you drive on a typical day and see how it fits your routine and lifestyle. Can you picture driving it for all occasions? ★*Tip: Typically, airport car rental locations have a large selection of rental cars.* If the model isn't available for rental, try to test-drive the car more than once at different times of day. Or verify with the dealer whether they would allow you to keep the car overnight.

Here are some more tips for selecting the car that's best for you:

- The exterior looks of a car might be important to you, but the interior design and feel should be more important. Look at it this way: While driving the car, you spend all your time inside it. So it makes sense to value the comfort of the interior over how the car looks on the outside.

- Horsepower may or may not be something that holds much importance for you. Different models of the same car can have higher or lower horsepower ratings. If horsepower matters at all to you, look up how much a car weighs. If two cars have the same horsepower but different weights, they can certainly feel different. Then again, two cars of similar weight and similar horsepower can feel different as well. So it ultimately comes down to how the car feels to you, regardless of the horsepower rating.

- Another point to keep in mind is traction. How well does the tire grip the road? It can depend on the type of tire, the size and how much tread is there. It can also depend on the car's weight distribution and whether it's an all-wheel-drive or two-wheel-drive vehicle. If a car has a lot of horsepower but struggles with traction, having that much power may not be very useful. Generally, an all-wheel or four-wheel-drive car should provide better traction (depending on the conditions). ★*Tip: For driving in winter/ snowy weather, winter tires can help with handling more than other tires.*

★*Tip: To get the most out of your car, read the owner's manual to become familiarized with it and learn all the features. For a new car, it's highly recommended that you follow the protocol for the break-in period as specified by the manufacturer or the owner's manual.*

Detailed Notes: _____

_____

_____

_____

_____

_____

_____

_____

_____

_____

_____

_____

_____

Detailed Notes: (continued) __

_____

_____

_____

_____

_____

_____

_____

_____

_____

_____

_____

_____

_____

_____

_____

_____

_____

_____